LET'S
see

Farms Long Ago

by Jennifer Blizin Gillis

Content Adviser: Susan Thompson, Agriculture Communications,
College of Agriculture, Iowa State University

Reading Adviser: Rosemary Palmer, Ph.D.,
Department of Literacy, College of Education,
Boise State University

Let's See Library
Compass Point Books
Minneapolis, Minnesota

Compass Point Books
3109 West 50th Street, #115
Minneapolis, MN 55410

Visit Compass Point Books on the Internet at *www.compasspointbooks.com*
or e-mail your request to *custserv@compasspointbooks.com*

On the cover: A farmer steers a plow that is pulled by horses.

Photographs ©: Index Stock Imagery, cover; Hulton/Archive by Getty Images, 4; Stock Montage, Inc., 6;
North Wind Picture Archives, 8, 14; U.S. Department of Agriculture/Russell Lee, 10, 12, 18; Library of
Congress, 16; Minnesota Historical Society/Corbis, 20.

Creative Director: Terri Foley
Managing Editor: Catherine Neitge
Editors: Brenda Haugen and Christianne Jones
Photo Researcher: Marcie C. Spence
Designers: Melissa Kes and Jaime Martens
Educational Consultant: Diane Smolinski

Library of Congress Cataloging-in-Publication Data
Gillis, Jennifer Blizin, 1950-
  Farms long ago / by Jennifer B. Gillis.
      p. cm. — (Let's see)
Includes bibliographical references (p.   ).
ISBN 0-7565-0671-9 (hardcover)
  1. Agriculture—History—Juvenile literature. 2. Farms—History—Juvenile literature.
  3. Farm life—History—Juvenile literature. I. Title. II. Series.
S519.G54 2004
630'.9—dc22   2003028219

Table of Contents

NOTE: In this book, words that are defined in the glossary
are in **bold** the first time they appear in the text.

A Farm Day

Farmers have always gotten up before sunrise. They would get up early so they could use every minute of daylight. Long ago, there was no electricity. Farmers lit **kerosene** lamps so they could see. They did many chores, such as milking cows or feeding animals, by lamplight.

When the sun came up in the summertime, farmers worked in their fields. They could only plow, plant, or pick crops while it was light outside. On long summer days, farmers often worked from 5 A.M. until 9 P.M. They called this "working from can't see to can't see."

◄ *A farm family poses outside their home in the 1880s.*

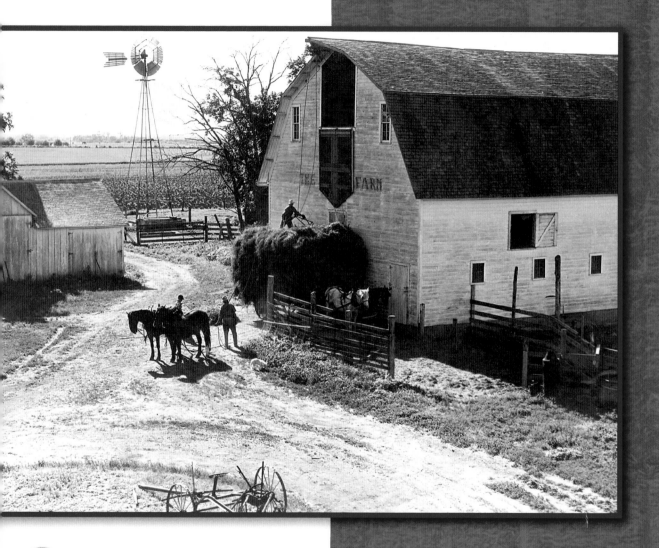

Farm Buildings

Today, many farm buildings are made of metal. Long ago, farm buildings were made of wood. The barn was the biggest building on the farm. Most barns had two floors. Animals lived in stalls on the first floor. Farmers kept hay for the animals upstairs in the **hayloft.**

Some farmers had **corncribs.** They were used to store whole ears of corn. The corncribs were made of **slats** with big spaces in between them. This let air into the corncrib to keep the corn from spoiling. Other farmers used tall **silos** to store **grains** such as wheat or oats.

◄ *A farmer puts hay in the top of his barn.*

Farm Tools

Long ago, most farmwork was done by hand. There was no plastic, so farm tools were made of wood and metal. These tools were heavy and took lots of energy to use. Farmers had axes to chop wood. Wood was used for cooking and heating.

In the field, farmers used **hoes** to break up clumps of dirt and keep weeds away from crops. They used **scythes** to cut down tall grasses or crops. They threw piles of hay or crops onto wagons with pitchforks.

◄ *This scene from an old calendar shows farmers with scythes and pitchforks.*

Getting Water

Water has always been important for people, crops, and animals. Long ago, it was harder to get. Water came from wells dug deep in the ground. Farmers got the water out of the wells by using pumps or by using buckets tied to ropes.

There often was no running water in farmhouses or buildings. When the farm family wanted to wash dishes or take baths, they brought in buckets of well water and heated it in a big pot on the stove. Then they could fill the sink or bathtub with hot water. Family members often bathed in the same water because getting more water and then heating it was such hard work.

◄ *A girl pumps water from a well in 1939.*

Planting and Picking Crops

Long ago, farmers had some simple machines to help with planting and picking crops. Most machines were pushed or pulled by animals.

Farmers used seed broadcasters to help plant crops. Farmers walked their fields turning the handles on these small machines. The seed broadcaster sprinkled seeds onto the ground.

At **harvest** time, the whole farm family had to help. They cut down or picked the crops by hand, then put them on carts or in wagons. It usually took more than one day to harvest a big crop.

◄ *Workers pick string beans in a field in the late 1930s.*

Farm Animals

Farmers kept large, heavy horses called draft horses. These animals could pull **plows** and heavy loads, such as piles of logs. Farmers also used mules to pull plows and carts.

Long ago, most farmers grew just enough to feed their families. They kept a few **beef** cows, pigs, chickens, and sheep. They drank milk from the **dairy** cows. They ate eggs from the chickens. Pigs and beef cows were made into meat. Farmers **sheared** the wool from sheep to make clothing. If they had any extra eggs, wool, or other farm products, farmers might sell them to make money.

◀ *A farm boy leads a team of horses while his father plows.*

Milking Cows

Long ago, farmers milked cows two times a day. They still do, but now there are machines that take milk from the cows. Long ago, farmers had to milk each cow by hand, often by lamplight.

The milk squirted into a pail. Cream would rise to the top of the pail. Then the cream would be made into butter or cheese.

Farmers used icehouses to store milk to drink. The icehouses kept the milk cold. On larger dairy farms, farmers put the milk into big cans and drove them to the train stations. Early-morning trains would take the milk to the cities.

◄ A woman milks a cow in the 1930s.

Hard Times on the Farm

It is not easy to make a living on a farm today. Long ago, it was even harder. Conditions had to be just perfect for the farm family to survive. Crops could die if there wasn't enough rain. It also might rain hard on a crop at harvest time and ruin it. Hailstorms could smash crops in the field. Insects could eat them up. Plant diseases could kill crops, too.

Sometimes the soil got worn out from planting crops that took too many **nutrients.** During the **Dust Bowl** in the 1930s, the soil on some farms dried up and began to blow away. Farmers and their families had to quit farming and move away.

◀ *Farm children sit in a doorway with their doll in Oklahoma during the Dust Bowl.*

Fun on the Farm

Farmers lived far from towns. Their neighbors were often miles away. There was no electricity, radio, TV, or video games. So, farm families often made parties out of work. They invited friends and neighbors to help them build a barn or harvest a crop. When the work was finished, everyone ate, played games, and had fun.

In winter, farm families had fun singing around the piano or making popcorn. In summer, they might sit outside and watch the fireflies. Life was harder long ago, but many people who lived then had happy memories. Maybe that is why they called them "the good old days."

◄ *A group of friends and neighbors gets together to build a barn in the early 1900s.*

Glossary

beef—meat from a cow, bull, or steer

corncribs—storage buildings for dried ears of corn that animals eat

dairy—relating to milk cows and milk products

Dust Bowl—the time during the 1930s when the soil in some states got worn out from dry weather and from planting too many crops that took away nutrients

grains—seeds from plants such as corn, wheat, oats, or barley

harvest—to gather crops

hayloft—the top floor of a barn where farmers keep hay for the animals to eat

hoes—tools with long handles and thin blades that are used to remove weeds and loosen soil

kerosene—a kind of gas that can be burned in lamps and stoves

nutrients—the materials a living thing needs to live and grow

plows—machines with metal blades that break up and turn over dirt

scythes—tools with handles and sharp, curved blades that are used to cut grass or crops

sheared—cut the wool off a sheep

silos—tall towers used to store grain

slats—thin strips of wood or metal

Did You Know?

• Most farms did not have bathrooms in the house. Toilets, called outhouses, were outside. People took baths in big metal tubs in the kitchen, near the stove.

• To keep food cold, farmers built icehouses out of stone or bricks. Part of the icehouse was under the ground. In winter, farmers cut ice from ponds and rivers. They wrapped it in hay and kept it in the icehouse.

Want to Know More?

In the Library

Artley, Bob. *Once Upon a Farm.* Gretna, La.: Pelican Publishing Co., 2000.

Bial, Raymond. *The Farms.* New York: Benchmark Books/Marshall Cavendish, 2002.

Longenecker, Theresa. *Who Grows Up on the Farm? A Book About Farm Animals and Their Offspring.* Minneapolis: Picture Window Books, 2003.

Wilkes, Angela. *A Farm Through Time.* New York: Dorling Kindersley, 2001.

On the Web

For more information on *farms long ago,* use FactHound to track down Web sites related to this book.

1. Go to *www.facthound.com*
2. Type in a search word related to this book or this book ID: 0756506719.
3. Click on the *Fetch It* button.

Your trusty FactHound will fetch the best Web sites for you!

On the Road

Living History Farms
2600 111th St.
Urbandale, IA 50322
515/278-5286
To take a tour of a working farm

Ardenwood Historic Farm
34600 Ardenwood Blvd.
Fremont, CA 94553
510/562-7275
To see how farming has changed through the years

Index

About the Author

Jennifer Blizin Gillis writes poetry and nonfiction books for children. She lives on a former dairy farm in Pittsboro, North Carolina, with her husband, a dog, and a cat. She is more of a gardener than a farmer, but has lived on farms and in farming communities.